Harry Potter™

WORLD
OF
STICKERS

EXPERIENCE THE WORLD OF HARRY POTTER AS IT HAS NEVER BEEN SEEN BEFORE

A vast, visual anthology of artwork inspired by major themes and elements from the films of Harry Potter, the art in this sticker book has been derived from an archive of style guides created exclusively by the creative team at Warner Bros. Originally conceived for branding and fashion, these designs have been carefully curated into this unique volume, delivering a magical museum of wizarding artwork.

This book has been organized in the order of art styles. If House crests were designed for a particular style, they will be the opening images for that section, followed by other Wizarding World icons inspired by the style.

In addition to uniquely designed Hogwarts house crests, discover the sticker versions of enchanting shop signs from Hogsmeade village, striking icons of the Ministry of Magic and the ominous Dark Mark, imaginatively lettered compositions of favorite film quotes, Quidditch-inspired banners and posters, detailed potion-bottle labels, glowing Patronus guardians, and much more.

This revised edition also features new sticker art included throughout the book. As a bonus to the stunning sticker collection, each image has also been printed in full color on the reverse side of the sticker pages, making this a keepsake book to be cherished and explored again and again.

FROM THE FILMS OF

Harry Potter ™

WORLD
OF
STICKERS

Art *from the* **Wizarding World Archive**

REVISED EDITION

THUNDER BAY
P · R · E · S · S
San Diego, California

GRYFFINDOR

SLYTHERIN

DRACO DORMIENS NUNQUAM TITILLANDUS

HUFFLEPUFF

RAVENCLAW

GRYFFINDOR

SLYTHERIN

DRACO DORMIENS NUNQUAM TITILLANDUS

HUFFLEPUFF

RAVENCLAW

GRYFFINDOR™

SLYTHERIN™

DRACO DORMIENS NUNQUAM TITILLANDUS

HUFFLEPUFF™

RAVENCLAW™

HUFFLEPUFF

DEDICATION

PATIENCE LOYALTY

GRYFFINDOR

BRAVERY COURAGE

DETERMINATION

RAVENCLAW

LEARNING WIT WISDOM

SLYTHERIN

AMBITION CUNNING

PRIDE

THE GOLDEN EGG

COME SEEK US WHERE OUR VOICES SOUND

HERBOLOGY GREENHOUSE

FORBIDDEN FOREST

HOME OF BANE

ROOM OF REQUIREMENT

HUFFLEPUFF

DEDICATION

PATIENCE · LOYALTY

GRYFFINDOR

BRAVERY · COURAGE

DETERMINATION

RAVENCLAW

LEARNING · WIT · WISDOM

SLYTHERIN

AMBITION · CUNNING

PRIDE

THE GOLDEN EGG

COME SEEK US WHERE OUR VOICES SOUND

HERBOLOGY GREENHOUSE

FORBIDDEN FOREST

HOME OF BANE

ROOM OF REQUIREMENT

PIERTOTUM LOCOMOTOR

EXPECTO PATRONUM

PIERTOTUM LOCOMOTOR

EXPECTO PATRONUM

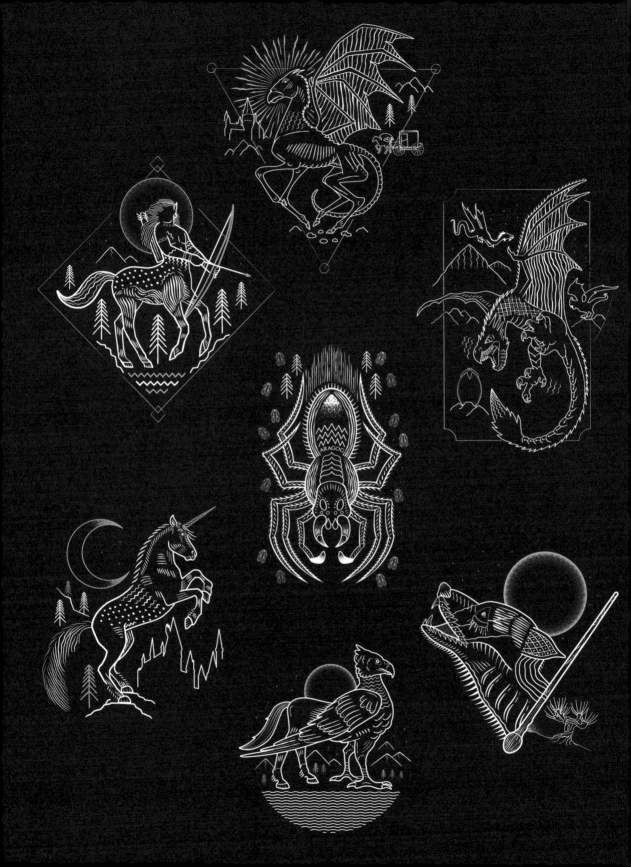

JUST BECAUSE YOU'RE ALLOWED TO USE MAGIC NOW DOES NOT MEAN YOU HAVE TO WHIP YOUR WANDS OUT FOR EVERYTHING!

The ones that love us NEVER REALLY LEAVE US IN HERE YOU CAN ALWAYS FIND THEM...

HORCRUX

YOU HAVE NOTHING TO FEAR IF YOU HAVE NOTHING TO HIDE

WORDS ARE, IN MY NOT-SO-HUMBLE OPINION, OUR MOST INEXHAUSTIBLE SOURCE OF MAGIC

always

Harry Potter

HUNGARIAN HORNTAIL

THE ELDER WAND
TOGETHER THEY MAKE THE DEATHLY HALLOWS
THE RESURRECTION STONE
TOGETHER THEY MAKE ONE MASTER OF DEATH
THE CLOAK OF INVISIBILITY

JUST BECAUSE **YOU'RE ALLOWED** TO USE **MAGIC** NOW **DOES NOT** MEAN YOU HAVE TO **WHIP YOUR WANDS OUT** FOR EVERYTHING!

The ones that love us NEVER REALLY LEAVE US IN HERE YOU CAN ALWAYS FIND THEM.

HORCRUX

YOU HAVE NOTHING TO **FEAR** IF YOU HAVE NOTHING TO **HIDE**

WORDS ARE, IN MY NOT-SO-HUMBLE OPINION, OUR MOST INEXHAUSTIBLE SOURCE OF **MAGIC**

always

HUNGARIAN HORNTAIL

THE ELDER WAND TOGETHER THEY MAKE ONE MASTER OF DEATH THE RESURRECTION STONE THE DEATHLY HALLOWS THE CLOAK OF INVISIBILITY

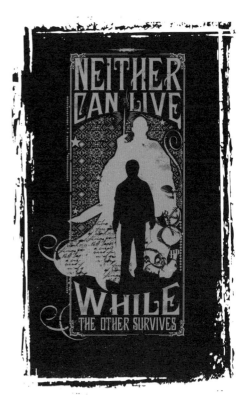

Hufflepuff

Ravenclaw

Dumbledore's
D.A

Room of
Requirement

Gryffindor

Slytherin

Hufflepuff

Ravenclaw

Dumbledore's Army

Room of Requirement

Gryffindor

Slytherin

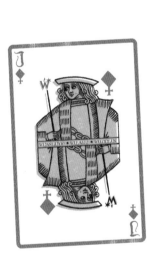

Hogwarts

Ravenclaw

Hufflepuff

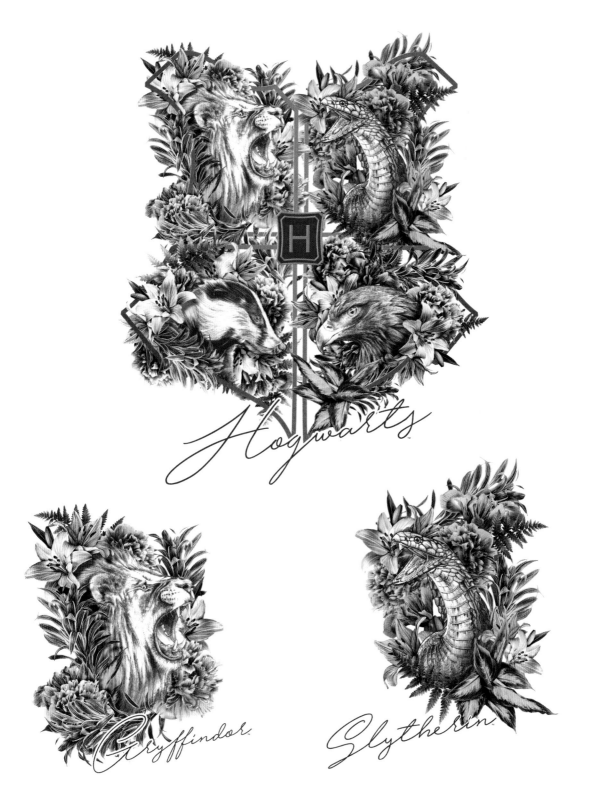

Hogwarts™

Gryffindor

Slytherin™

Hogwarts

Ravenclaw

Hufflepuff

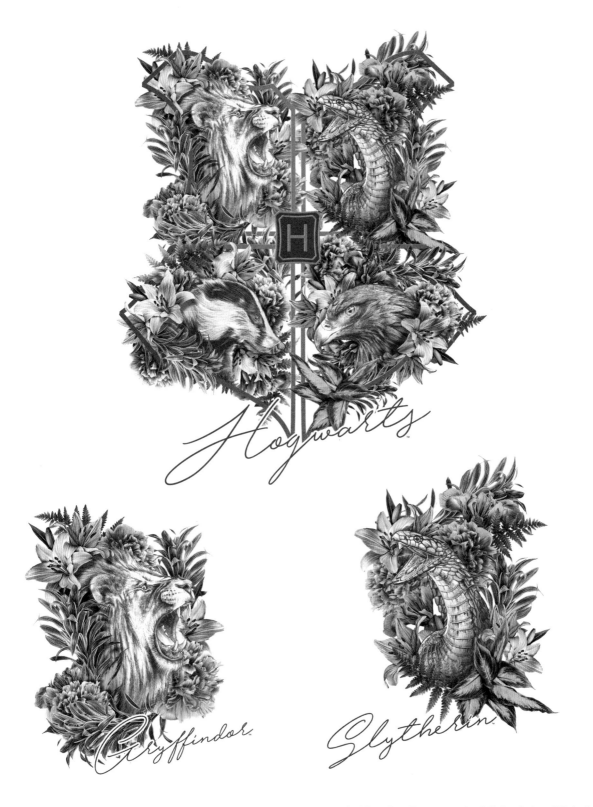

Hogwarts™

Gryffindor™

Slytherin™

MORSMORDRE

THE DARK MARK

MAGICAL CREATURES

HE WHO MUST NOT BE NAMED

Incendio

VOLDEMORT

MAGICAL CREATURES

LordVoldemort

DURMSTRANG

FAWKES

FAWKES

Voldemort

Stupefy

The DARK MARK

Incendio

MORSMORDRE

THE DARK MARK

MAGICAL CREATURES

HE WHO MUST NOT BE NAMED

Incendio

VOLDEMORT

MAGICAL CREATURES

Lord Voldemort

DURMSTRANG

FAWKES

FAWKES

Voldemort

Stupefy

The DARK MARK

Incendio

D.M

Durmstrang

Voldemort

Morsmordre

The Unbreakable Vow

Beauxbatons

STUPEFY

Avada Kedavra

MORSMORDRE

Lord Voldemort

CRUCIATUS

D.M

Duimstrang

Voldemort

MORSMORDRE

The UNBREAKABLE VOW

Beauxbatons

STUPEFY

MORSMORDRE

Lord
Voldemort

GRYFFINDOR

SLYTHERIN

HUFFLEPUFF

HOGWARTS

RAVENCLAW

GRYFFINDOR

SLYTHERIN

RAVENCLAW

HUFFLEPUFF

GRYFFINDOR

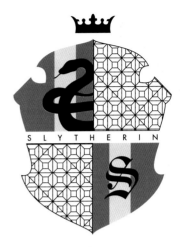

SLYTHERIN

HOGWARTS

HUFFLEPUFF

RAVENCLAW

GRYFFINDOR

SLYTHERIN

HUFFLEPUFF

HOGWARTS

RAVENCLAW

GRYFFINDOR

SLYTHERIN

RAVENCLAW

HUFFLEPUFF

GRYFFINDOR

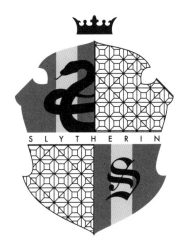

SLYTHERIN

HOGWARTS

HUFFLEPUFF

RAVENCLAW

DOBBY IS FREE

DOBBY

DOBBY
—HAS NO—
MASTER
DOBBY
—IS A—
FREE
ELF

Dobby
HAS NO MASTER
DOBBY
IS A FREE ELF

Free Dobby

FREE
THE HOUSE-
ELVES

S.P.E.W.
SOCIETY FOR THE PROMOTION OF ELFISH WELFARE

DOBBY
HAS COME TO SAVE HARRY POTTER AND HIS FRIENDS

DOBBY IS FREE

DOBBY HAS NO MASTER DOBBY IS A FREE ELF

DOBBY

Dobby HAS NO MASTER DOBBY IS A FREE ELF

Free Dobby

FREE THE HOUSE-ELVES

S.P.E.W.
SOCIETY FOR THE PROMOTION OF ELFISH WELFARE

DOBBY
HAS COME TO SAVE HARRY POTTER AND HIS FRIENDS

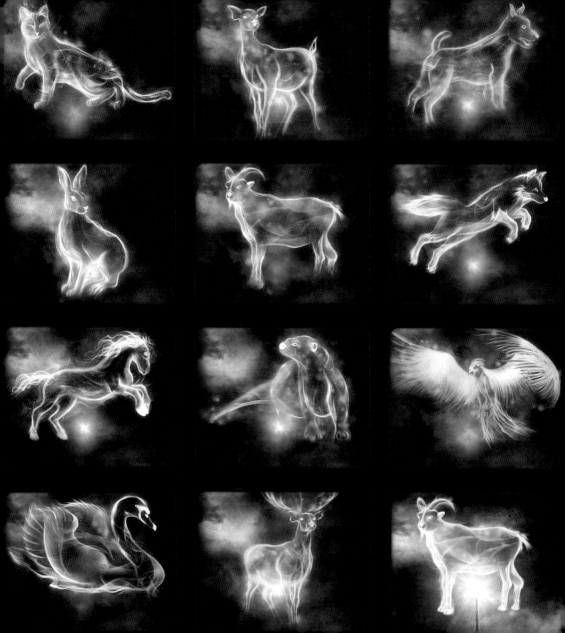

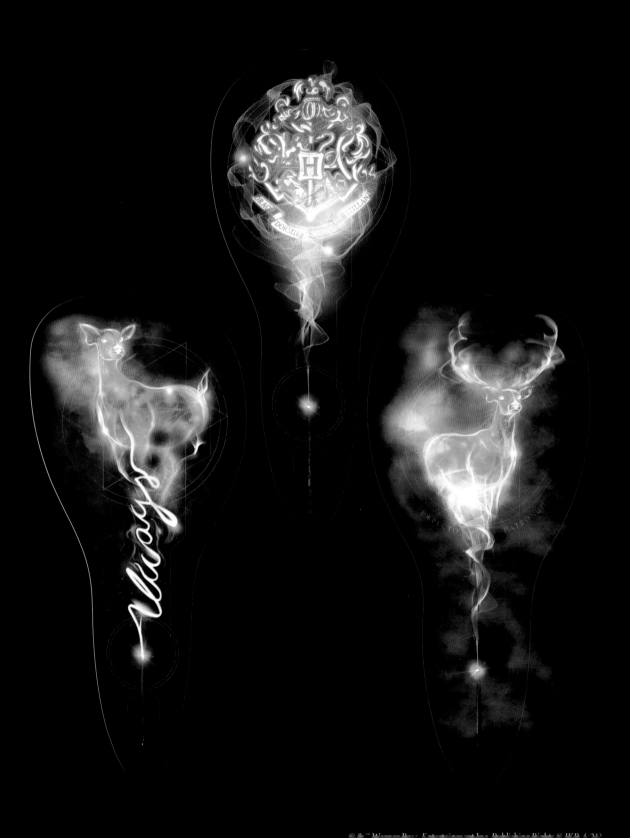

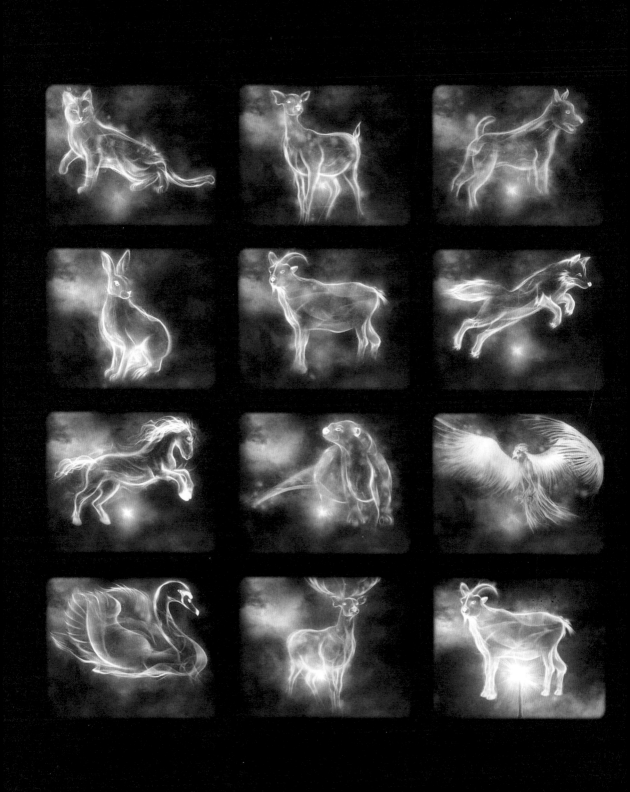

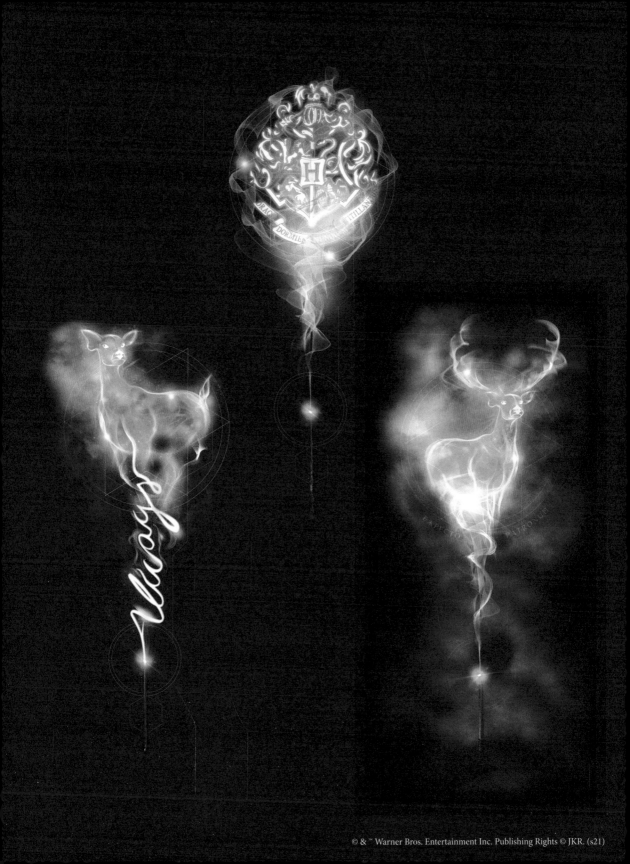

I SOLEMNLY SWEAR

I AM UP TO NO GOOD

THE ORDER of THE PHOENIX

MORSMORDRE

EXPECTO PATRONUM

HOGWARTS

DA
DUMBLEDORE'S ARMY

SLYTHERIN

GRYFFINDOR

RAVENCLAW

HUFFLEPUFF

GRYFFINDOR

HOGWARTS

SLYTHERIN

HUFFLEPUFF

RAVENCLAW

Hogwarts Castle

Hogwarts Express

I SOLEMNLY SWEAR

I AM UP TO NO GOOD

THE ORDER OF THE PHOENIX

MORSMORDRE

EXPECTO PATRONUM

HOGWARTS

DA

DUMBLEDORE'S ARMY

SLYTHERIN

GRYFFINDOR

RAVENCLAW

HUFFLEPUFF

GRYFFINDOR

HOGWARTS

SLYTHERIN

HUFFLEPUFF

RAVENCLAW

Hogwarts Castle

Hogwarts Express

GRYFFINDOR

SLYTHERIN

HUFFLEPUFF

RAVENCLAW

GRYFFINDOR

SLYTHERIN

HUFFLEPUFF

RAVENCLAW

RAVENCLAW

SLYTHERIN

GRYFFINDOR

HUFFLEPUFF

HOGWARTS

DRACO DORMIENS NUNQUAM TITILLANDUS

LET THE MATCH BEGIN!

Harry Potter

ORDER OF THE PHOENIX

THE THINGS WE LOSE HAVE A WAY OF COMING BACK TO US IN THE END

RAVENCLAW

SLYTHERIN

GRYFFINDOR

HUFFLEPUFF

HOGWARTS

H

DRACO DORMIENS NUNQUAM TITILLANDUS

LET THE MATCH BEGIN!

Harry Potter

ORDER OF THE PHOENIX

THE THINGS WE LOSE HAVE A WAY OF COMING BACK TO US IN THE END

POTTER 07

GRYFFINDOR
· Team Quidditch ·
PROPERTY OF HOGWARTS. SCHOOL OF WITCHCRAFT AND WIZARDRY

Gryffindor 07

Team Quidditch

GRYFFINDOR

TOP SCORE GRYFFINDOR!

GRYFFINDOR Quidditch KEEPER 02

G. WEASLEY 05
PROPERTY OF HOGWARTS. SCHOOL OF WITCHCRAFT AND WIZARDRY

Gryffindor Captain

R. WEASLEY 02
PROPERTY OF HOGWARTS. SCHOOL OF WITCHCRAFT AND WIZARDRY

Gryffindor R. WEASLEY KEEPER

GRYFFINDOR
PROPERTY OF HOGWARTS. SCHOOL OF WITCHCRAFT AND WIZARDRY

KEEPER GRYFFINDOR

GRYFFINDOR

YOU CAN SCORE GRYFFINDOR!

Gryffindor

R. WEASLEY
02
Keeper

G. Weasley
05
GRYFFINDOR

H. POTTER
Seeker
07

H. POTTER
07
PROPERTY OF HOGWARTS SCHOOL OF WITCHCRAFT AND WIZARDRY

GRYFFINDOR
CAPTAIN
H. POTTER

H. POTTER
07

CAPTAIN
Gryffindor

Gryffindor

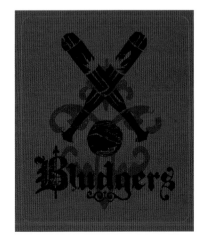

Bludgers

POTTER 07

GRYFFINDOR

Team Quidditch

PROPERTY OF HOGWARTS.SCHOOL OF WITCHCRAFT AND WIZARDRY

Gryffindor™ 07

Team Quidditch

GRYFFINDOR

TOP SCORE GRYFFINDOR!

GRYFFINDOR Quidditch KEEPER 02

G. WEASLEY 05

PROPERTY OF HOGWARTS.SCHOOL OF WITCHCRAFT AND WIZARDRY

Gryffindor C Captain

R. WEASLEY 02

PROPERTY OF HOGWARTS.SCHOOL OF WITCHCRAFT AND WIZARDRY

Gryffindor R. WEASLEY KEEPER

GRYFFINDOR™
PROPERTY OF HOGWARTS.SCHOOL OF WITCHCRAFT AND WIZARDRY

KEEPER GRYFFINDOR

GRYFFINDOR

YOU CAN SCORE GRYFFINDOR!

Gryffindor

R. WEASLEY
02
Keeper
GRYFFINDOR

G. Weasley
05
GRYFFINDOR

H. POTTER
Seeker
07

H. POTTER
07

PROPERTY OF HOGWARTS SCHOOL OF WITCHCRAFT AND WIZARDRY

GRYFFINDOR
CAPTAIN
H. POTTER

H. POTTER
07

GRYFFINDOR
CAPTAIN
Gryffindor

Gryffindor

Bludgers

LOVE POTION · LOVE POTION

ALL POSTS ARE OPEN!

TRY Quidditch GO FLYING TODAY!

PUT YOUR NAME IN THE... GOBLET OF FIRE!

WE GOT FIREWORKS!

TRIWIZARD TOURNAMENT

JOIN S.P.E.W.

FREE THE HOUSE-ELVES!

WEASLEYS' WIZARD wheezes

ONLY FOUND AT:

93 DIAGON ALLEY

COURAGE · BRAVERY · DETERMINATION
Gryffindor
PREFECT

PRIDE · AMBITION · CUNNING
Slytherin
PREFECT

DEDICATION · PATIENCE · LOYALTY
Hufflepuff
PREFECT

WIT · LEARNING · WISDOM
Ravenclaw
PREFECT

LOVE POTION · LOVE POTION

ALL POSTS ARE OPEN!

TRY Quidditch GO FLYING TODAY!

PUT YOUR NAME IN THE... GOBLET OF FIRE!

WE GOT FIREWORKS!

JOIN S.P.E.W.!

FREE THE HOUSE-ELVES!

TRIWIZARD TOURNAMENT

WEASLEYS' WIZARD wheezes

ONLY FOUND AT:

93 DIAGON ALLEY

COURAGE • BRAVERY • DETERMINATION

Gryffindor

PREFECT

PRIDE • AMBITION • CUNNING

Slytherin

PREFECT

DEDICATION • PATIENCE • LOYALTY

Hufflepuff

PREFECT

WIT • LEARNING • WISDOM

Ravenclaw

PREFECT

HUFFLEPUFF

POLYJUICE

AMORTENTIA

VERITASERUM

POTIONS

RAVENCLAW

SLYTHERIN

GRYFFINDOR

RAVENCLAW

SLYTHERIN

(HOGWARTS SCHOOL OF WITCHCRAFT AND WIZARDRY)

DIVINATION

THE MOST DIFFICULT OF ALL MAGICAL ARTS
-SYBILL PATRICIA TRELAWNEY

(Mandragora)

MANDRAKE

WARNING!
Earmuffs
must be
warn

The root
of the mandrake
can be used to
revive those who
have been
Petrified

POLYJUICE

AMORTENTIA

VERITASERUM

POTIONS

(HOGWARTS SCHOOL OF WITCHCRAFT AND WIZARDRY)

DIVINATION

THE MOST DIFFICULT OF ALL MAGICAL ARTS
·SYBILL PATRICIA TRELAWNEY·

(Mandragora)

MANDRAKE

WARNING!
Earmuffs
must be
warn

The root
of the mandrake
can be used to
revive those who
have been
Petrified

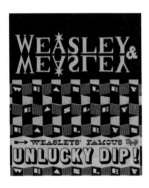

JUMPING SNAKES

WEASLEY AND WEASLEY

GHASTLY GARROTING GRASS SNAKES

L.150

WEASLEY & WEASLEY

Weasley & Weasley

Weasley

AUTHENTIC

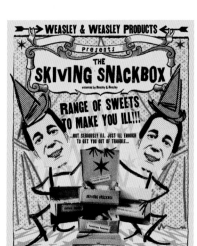

WEASLEY & WEASLEY PRODUCTS

presents

THE SKIVING SNACKBOX

patented by Weasley & Weasley

RANGE OF SWEETS TO MAKE YOU ILL!!!

...NOT SERIOUSLY ILL. JUST ILL ENOUGH TO GET YOU OUT OF TROUBLE...

SAVE MONEY NOW! 3 BOXES FOR THE PRICE OF 2 FREE DELIVERY ON ALL OWL POST ORDERS

WEASLEY & WEASLEY

THIS WEEK'S MANAGERS' SPECIALS!

"DECOY DETONATOR"
BUY ONE, GET A SCREAMING YO-YO FOR A BIT LESS THAN YOU EXPECTED!

"NOSE-BITING TEACUP"
TEA-PARTY SPECIAL! 4 FOR 3! CHEEKY TEAS - GUARANTEED TO TEASE!

"SELF-WRITING QUILLS"
FREE WITH EVERY PURCHASE TODAY - THE NOVEL CYRILLIC MODEL

BACK BY POPULAR DEMAND- "JINX-OFF!"
why pay 1 galleon,16 sickles,28 knuts for each item?
RELAX IN TOTAL SPELL-PROTECTION - FULL KIT -4 galleons,16 sickles,28 knuts!

PROPER PRODUCT

WEASLEY & WEASLEY

Weasleys' WONDROUS Wands

Weasleys' WONDROUS Wands

L.150

BOX O'ROCKETS

CONTAINS 10 ROCKETS WEASLEY & WEASLEY

WEASLEY AND WEASLEY

JUMPING
SNAKES

GHASTLY GARROTING GRASS SNAKES

L.150

WEASLEY & WEASLEY

Weasley & Weasley

Weasley

AUTHENTIC

→ WEASLEY & WEASLEY PRODUCTS ←

Presents

THE

SKIVING SNACKBOX

presented by Weasley & Weasley

RANGE OF SWEETS
TO MAKE YOU ILL!!!

...NOT SERIOUSLY ILL, JUST ILL ENOUGH
TO GET YOU OUT OF TROUBLE...

SAVE MONEY NOW! 3 BOXES FOR THE PRICE OF 2
FREE DELIVERY ON ALL OWL POST ORDERS

WEASLEY & WEASLEY

THIS WEEK'S
MANAGERS' SPECIALS!

"DECOY DETONATOR"
BUY ONE, GET A SCREAMING YO-YO
FOR A BIT LESS THAN YOU EXPECTED!

"NOSE-BITING TEACUP"
TEA-PARTY SPECIAL! 4 FOR 3!
CHEEKY TEAS - GUARANTEED TO TEASE!

"SELF-WRITING QUILLS"
FREE WITH EVERY PURCHASE TODAY -
THE NOVEL CYRILLIC MODEL

BACK BY POPULAR DEMAND-
☞ "JINX-OFF!" ☜
why pay 1 galleon, 16 sickles, 28 knuts for each item?
RELAX IN TOTAL SPELL-PROTECTION -
FULL KIT -4 galleons, 16 sickles, 28 knuts!

PROPER PRODUCT

WEASLEY & WEASLEY

**Weasleys'
WONDROUS
★ Wands ★**

weasleys'
WONDROUS
★Wands★

weasleys

L.150

BOX O'ROCKETS

CONTAINS 10 ROCKETS WEASLEY & WEASLEY

GRYFFINDOR

SLYTHERIN

HOGWARTS

DRACO DORMIENS NUNQUAM TITILLANDUS

HUFFLEPUFF

RAVENCLAW

HOGWARTS

A PROUD MEMBER OF DUMBLEDORE'S ARMY

I WOULD RATHER BE AT HOGWARTS

WAITING FOR MY LETTER FROM HOGWARTS

GRYFFINDOR

SLYTHERIN

HOGWARTS

DRACO DORMIENS NUNQUAM TITILLANDUS

HUFFLEPUFF

RAVENCLAW

HOGWARTS

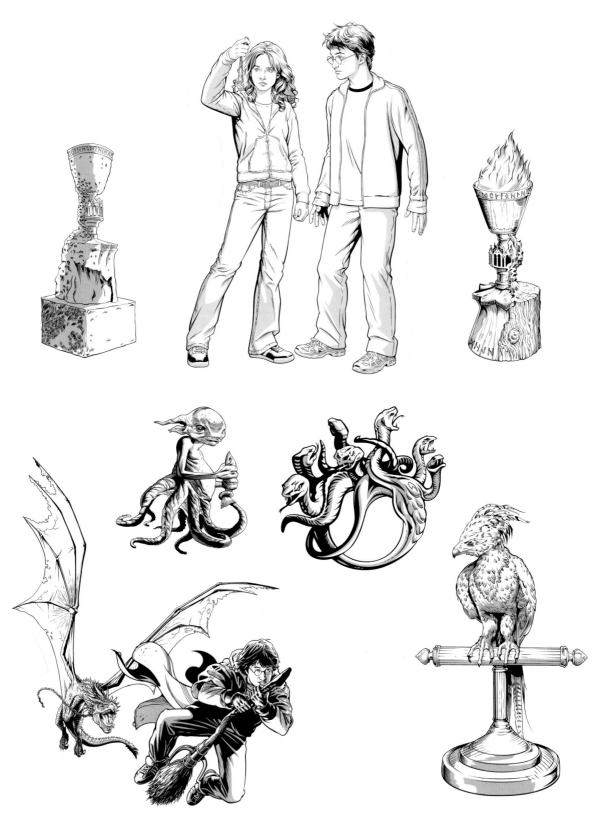

THREE BROTHERS

LONGING

POWER

HUMILITY

THE DEATHLY HALLOWS

GRYFFINDOR

COURAGE

DETERMINATION

BRAVERY

SLYTHERIN

AMBITION

CUNNING

PRIDE

THREE BROTHERS

LONGING

POWER

HUMILITY

THE DEATHLY HALLOWS

GRYFFINDOR

COURAGE

DETERMINATION

BRAVERY

SLYTHERIN

AMBITION

CUNNING

PRIDE

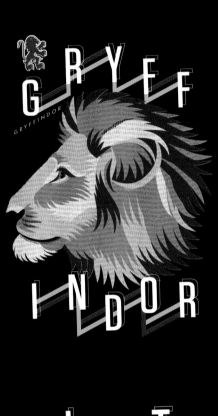

GRYFF

INDOR

GRYFFINDOR

RAVEN

CLAW

RAVENCLAW

SLYTH

ERIN

SLYTHERIN

HUFFLE

PUFF

HUFFLEPUFF

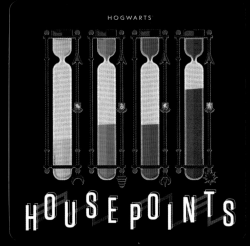

GRYFFINDOR

RAVENCLAW

SLYTHERIN

HUFFLEPUFF

GOLDEN SNITCH

QUIDDITCH

QUAFFLES

BLUDGERS

QUIDDITCH

QUIDDITCH

TRI WIZARD CUP

TRI WIZARD CUP

HOGWARTS

HOUSE POINTS

QUIDDITCH

GOLDEN SNITCH

QUAFFLES

BLUDGERS

EMERGENCY TRANSPORT FOR THE STRANDED WITCH OR WIZARD

THE
**Knight
Bus**

ALL ABOARD THE
**HOGWARTS
EXPRESS**

PLATFORM 9¾

· LONDON TO HOGSMEADE ·

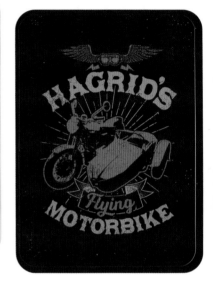

HAGRID'S

Flying

MOTORBIKE

PLATFORM $9\frac{3}{4}$

HAGRID'S
Flying
MOTORBIKE

HOGWARTS EXPRESS

THE
Knight
Bus

ALL ABOARD THE
HOGWARTS
EXPRESS

PLATFORM 9¾

·LONDON TO HOGSMEADE·

HAGRID'S
Flying
MOTORBIKE

PLATFORM $9\frac{3}{4}$

HAGRID'S *Flying* MOTORBIKE

HOGWARTS EXPRESS

HOGWARTS

HOGWARTS

GRYFFINDOR

HUFFLEPUFF

SLYTHERIN

RAVENCLAW

GRYFFINDOR

COURAGE DETERMINATION BRAVERY

GRYFFINDOR

G

COURAGE DETERMINATION BRAVERY

HUFFLEPUFF

HUFFLEPUFF

DEDICATION PATIENCE LOYALTY

SLYTHERIN

PRIDE AMBITION CUNNING

SLYTHERIN

PRIDE
AMBITION
CUNNING

RAVENCLAW

LEARNING WIT WISDOM

RAVENCLAW

WIT LEARNING WISDOM

HOGWARTS EXPRESS 5972

GRYFFINDOR
COURAGE DETERMINATION BRAVERY

HUFFLEPUFF
DEDICATION PATIENCE LOYALTY

QUIDDITCH

G H S R

HOGWARTS

SLYTHERIN
PRIDE AMBITION CUNNING

RAVENCLAW
WIT LEARNING WISDOM

CREATURES

GRYFFINDOR

HUFFLEPUFF

SLYTHERIN

RAVENCLAW

GRYFFINDOR

COURAGE DETERMINATION BRAVERY

GRYFFINDOR

COURAGE DETERMINATION BRAVERY

HUFFLEPUFF

HUFFLEPUFF

DEDICATION PATIENCE LOYALTY

SLYTHERIN

PRIDE AMBITION CUNNING

SLYTHERIN

PRIDE
AMBITION
CUNNING

RAVENCLAW

RAVENCLAW

WIT LEARNING WISDOM

HOGWARTS EXPRESS: 5972

GRYFFINDOR

COURAGE   DETERMINATION   BRAVERY

HUFFLEPUFF

DEDICATION   PATIENCE   LOYALTY

QUIDDITCH

HOGWARTS

SLYTHERIN

PRIDE   AMBITION   CUNNING

RAVENCLAW

WIT   LEARNING   WISDOM

CREATURES

HOGWARTS

HOGWARTS
SCHOOL OF WITCHCRAFT & WIZARDRY
FLYING LESSONS

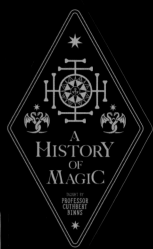

A
HISTORY
OF
MAGIC

TAUGHT BY
PROFESSOR
CUTHBERT
BINNS

— HOGWARTS —
POTIONS
The subtle science and exact art
CLASSES

Taught by   SEVERUS
                   SNAPE

SCHOOL OF WITCHCRAFT & WIZARDRY

Care of
MAGICAL
CREATURES
HOGWARTS
SCHOOL OF WITCHCRAFT
& WIZARDRY

DEFENSIVE SPELLS · RIDDIKULUS · EXPECTO PATRONUM · EXPELLIARMUS
DEFENCE AGAINST
THE DARK ARTS
HOGWARTS
SCHOOL OF WITCHCRAFT
& WIZARDRY
BOGGARTS · PATRONUSES · GRINDYLOWS · RED CAPS · KAPPAS · HINKYPUNKS

Swish & flick!
CHARMS
CLASSES
WITH
PROFESSOR
FLITWICK

HOGWARTS
SCHOOL OF WITCHCRAFT & WIZARDRY
H F H L
FLYING LESSONS

A
HISTORY
OF
MAGIC
TAUGHT BY
PROFESSOR
CUTHBERT
BINNS

— HOGWARTS —
POTIONS
The subtle science and exact art
CLASSES
Taught by   SEVERUS
                   SNAPE
SCHOOL OF WITCHCRAFT & WIZARDRY

Care of
MAGICAL
CREATURES
HOGWARTS
SCHOOL OF WITCHCRAFT
& WIZARDRY

DEFENSIVE SPELLS · RIDDIKULUS · EXPECTO PATRONUM · EXPELLIARMUS
DEFENCE AGAINST
THE DARK ARTS
HOGWARTS
SCHOOL OF WITCHCRAFT
& WIZARDRY
BOGGARTS · PATRONUSES · GRINDYLOWS · RED CAPS · KAPPAS · HINKYPUNKS

Swish & flick!
CHARMS
CLASSES
WITH
PROFESSOR
FLITWICK

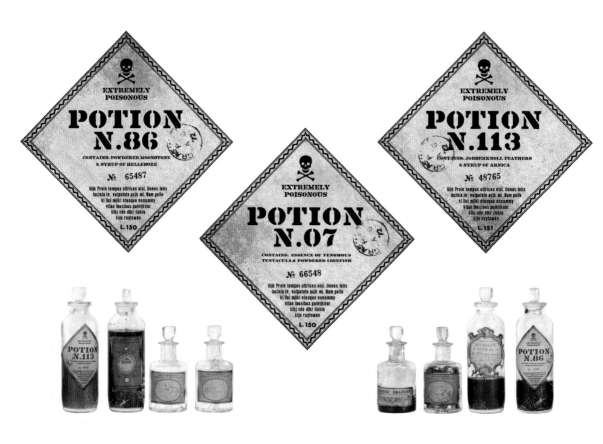

SOPOPHOROUS

028370

FROM THE APOTHECARIUM OF HORACE E. F. SLUGHORN

MANDRAKE ELIXIR

39423

FROM THE APOTHECARIUM OF HORACE E. F. SLUGHORN

LACEWING FLIES

A0752

FROM THE APOTHECARIUM OF HORACE E. F. SLUGHORN

PORCUPINE PARTS

L.50

FROM THE APOTHECARIUM OF HORACE E. F. SLUGHORN

BUNDIMUN POTION

08 SET 1472
Nº 2598

FROM THE APOTHECARIUM OF HORACE E. F. SLUGHORN

DEFLATING DRAUGHT

Nº 99810

FROM THE APOTHECARIUM OF HORACE E. F. SLUGHORN

MIXTURE
No.74

HORNED SLUGS

MIXTURE

SELD.

No. *004*

Each mixture contains:

Horned Slugs.................25 fl.oz
Tartar arnica..................17 fl.oz
Milk of Magnesia............21 fl.oz
Witch Hazel....................30 fl.oz
Epsom Salts....................26 fl.oz
Dried Slugs.....................12 fl.oz

Please handle this mixture with care. Keep lid closed at all times. In case of contact with skin wash immediately with Mrs. Skower's All-Purpose Magical Mess Remover.

POLYJUICE POTION

A0052

FROM THE APOTHECARIUM OF HORACE F. SLUGHORN

KEEP LID CLOSED AT ALL TIMES

SLEEPING DRAUGHT

A0075

FROM THE APOTHECARIUM OF HORACE F. SLUGHORN

KEEP LID CLOSED AT ALL TIMES

FROM THE APOTHECARIUM OF
HORACE E. F. SLUGHORN

CC
61042

MIXTURE
No.83

RAT SPLEEN

MIXTURE

VOLG
ARNILOT

No. *006*

Each mixture contains:

Rat Spleen.......................15 fl.oz
Kneazle hair....................09 fl.oz
Avocado skin...................14 fl.oz
Shrake spikes..................28 fl.oz
Knotgrass........................34 fl.oz
Gurdyroot.......................39 fl.oz

Please handle this mixture with care. Keep lid closed at all times. In case of contact with skin wash immediately with Mrs. Skower's All-Purpose Magical Mess Remover.

LACEWING FLIES

A0752

FROM THE APOTHECARIUM OF HORACE F. SLUGHORN

KEEP LID CLOSED AT ALL TIMES

BOOMSLANG SKIN

A0002

FROM THE APOTHECARIUM OF HORACE F. SLUGHORN

KEEP LID CLOSED AT ALL TIMES

FROM THE APOTHECARIUM OF
HORACE E. F. SLUGHORN

CC
61042

MIXTURE
No.42

ARMADILLO BILE

MIXTURE

No. *440*

Each mixture contains:

Bat wings........................19 fl.oz
Armadillo Bile.................20 fl.oz
Wormwood.....................16 fl.oz
Amortentia......................31 fl.oz
Acromantula Venom......02 fl.oz
Aconite............................09 fl.oz

Please handle this mixture with care. Keep lid closed at all times. In case of contact with skin wash immediately with Mrs. Skower's All-Purpose Magical Mess Remover.

MIXTURE
No.51

FROG PARTS

MIXTURE

Amonynshy
Margomtist
orum

No. *606*

Each mixture contains:

Frog tongue.....................08 fl.oz
Arnica Gel........................21 fl.oz
Asphodel..........................30 fl.oz
Wild Lettuce....................12 fl.oz
Fluxweed.........................41 fl.oz
Slug juice.........................39 fl.oz

Please handle this mixture with care. Keep lid closed at all times. In case of contact with skin wash immediately with Mrs. Skower's All-Purpose Magical Mess Remover.

MIXTURE
No.34

SCARAB BEETLE

MIXTURE

ORGLATOX
SEPP
ELOX VE PANCHOX
SARG.

No. *460*

Each mixture contains:

Beetle wings....................20 fl.oz
Tartar emetic...................18 fl.oz
Eobelia.............................17 fl.oz
Ginger root......................10 fl.oz
Lacewing flies.................36 fl.oz
Dried leeches...................58 fl.oz

Please handle this mixture with care. Keep lid closed at all times. In case of contact with skin wash immediately with Mrs. Skower's All-Purpose Magical Mess Remover.

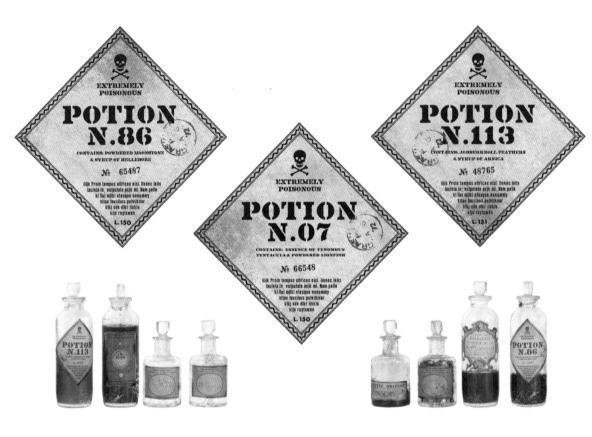

SOPOPHOROUS

028370

FROM THE APOTHECARIUM OF HORACE E. F. SLUGHORN

MANDRAKE ELIXIR

39423

FROM THE APOTHECARIUM OF HORACE E. F. SLUGHORN

LACEWING FLIES

A0752

FROM THE APOTHECARIUM OF HORACE E. F. SLUGHORN

PORCUPINE PARTS

L.50

FROM THE APOTHECARIUM OF HORACE E. F. SLUGHORN

BUNDIMUN POTION

08 SEP 1972
No 2598

FROM THE APOTHECARIUM OF HORACE E. F. SLUGHORN

DEFLATING DRAUGHT

No 99810

FROM THE APOTHECARIUM OF HORACE E. F. SLUGHORN

MIXTURE
No. 74

HORNED SLUGS
MIXTURE

SELD.

No. *004*

Each mixture contains:

Horned Slugs...............25 fl.oz
Tartar arnica................17fl.oz
Milk of Magnesia..........21 fl.oz
Witch Hazel.................30 fl.oz
Epsom Salts.................26 fl.oz
Dried Slugs..................12 fl.oz

Please handle this mixture with care. Keep lid closed at all
times. In case of contact with skin wash immediately with
Mrs. Skower's All-Purpose Magical Mess Remover.

POLYJUICE POTION

A 0 0 5 2

FROM THE APOTHECARIUM OF HORACE E. F. SLUGHORN

KEEP LID CLOSED AT ALL TIMES

SLEEPING DRAUGHT

A 0 0 7 5

FROM THE APOTHECARIUM OF HORACE E. SLUGHORN

KEEP LID CLOSED AT ALL TIMES

FROM THE APOTHECARIUM OF
HORACE E. F. SLUGHORN

CC
61042

MIXTURE
No. 83

RAT
SPLEEN
MIXTURE

VOLG
ARNILOT

No. *006*

Each mixture contains:

Rat Spleen...................15 fl.oz
Kneazle hair................09 fl.oz
Avocado skin...............14 fl.oz
Shrake spikes...............28 fl.oz
Knotgrass....................34 fl.oz
Gurdyroot....................39 fl.oz

Please handle this mixture with care. Keep lid closed at all
times. In case of contact with skin wash immediately with
Mrs. Skower's All-Purpose Magical Mess Remover.

LACEWING FLIES

A 0 7 5 2

FROM THE APOTHECARIUM OF HORACE E. F. SLUGHORN

KEEP LID CLOSED AT ALL TIMES

BOOMSLANG SKIN

A 0 0 0 2

FROM THE APOTHECARIUM OF HORACE E. SLUGHORN

KEEP LID CLOSED AT ALL TIMES

FROM THE APOTHECARIUM OF
HORACE E. F. SLUGHORN

37

CC
61042

MIXTURE
No. 42

ARMADILLO
BILE
MIXTURE

No. *440*

Each mixture contains:

Bat wings....................19 fl.oz
Armadillo Bile.............20 fl.oz
Wormwood..................16 fl.oz
Amortentia..................31 fl.oz
Acromantula Venom....02 fl.oz
Aconite........................09 fl.oz

Please handle this mixture with care. Keep lid closed at all
times. In case of contact with skin wash immediately with
Mrs. Skower's All-Purpose Magical Mess Remover.

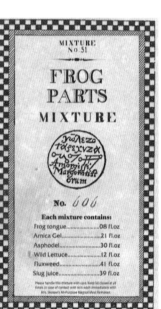

MIXTURE
No. 51

FROG
PARTS
MIXTURE

No. *606*

Each mixture contains:

Frog tongue..................08 fl.oz
Arnica Gel....................21 fl.oz
Asphodel.......................30 fl.oz
Wild Lettuce.................12 fl.oz
Fluxweed......................41 fl.oz
Slug Juice......................39 fl.oz

Please handle this mixture with care. Keep lid closed at all
times. In case of contact with skin wash immediately with
Mrs. Skower's All-Purpose Magical Mess Remover.

MIXTURE
No. 34

SCARAB
BEETLE
MIXTURE

No. *460*

Each mixture contains:

Beetle wings...................20 fl.oz
Tartar emetic..................18 fl.oz
Eobella..........................17 fl.oz
Ginger root....................10 fl.oz
Lacewing flies................30 fl.oz
Dried leeches.................58 fl.oz

Please handle this mixture with care. Keep lid closed at all
times. In case of contact with skin wash immediately with
Mrs. Skower's All-Purpose Magical Mess Removal.

Hogwarts

OWL POST

HOGWARTS EXPRESS

Chocolate Frog

HAPPEE BIRTH DAE HARRY

LOVE POTION

GRYFFINDOR

RAVENCLAW

SLYTHERIN

HUFFLEPUFF

Hogwarts

GRYFFINDOR

RAVENCLAW

SLYTHERIN

HUFFLEPUFF

GRYFFINDOR

HUFFLEPUFF

SLYTHERIN

RAVENCLAW

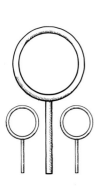

DRACO DORMIENS NUNQUAM TITILLANDUS

FIRST YEAR

HOGWARTS SCHOOL

QUAFFLE

QUIDDITCH AT HOGWARTS

BLUDGER

GOLDEN SNITCH

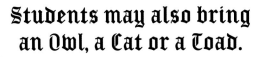

Students may also bring an Owl, a Cat or a Toad.

1 Wand

1 Cauldron
(pewter, standard size 2)

1 set of glass or
crystal phials

1 telescope

1 set of
brass scales

SPELLS
&
CHARMS

GRYFFINDOR

HUFFLEPUFF

SLYTHERIN

RAVENCLAW

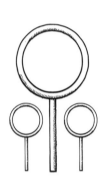

DRACO DORMIENS NUNQUAM TITILLANDUS

FIRST YEAR
HOGWARTS SCHOOL

QUAFFLE QUIDDITCH AT HOGWARTS BLUDGER
GOLDEN SNITCH

Students may also bring an Owl, a Cat or a Toad.

1 Wand

1 Cauldron
(pewter, standard size 2)

1 set of glass or
crystal phials

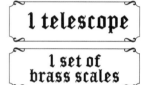

1 telescope

1 set of
brass scales

SPELLS & CHARMS

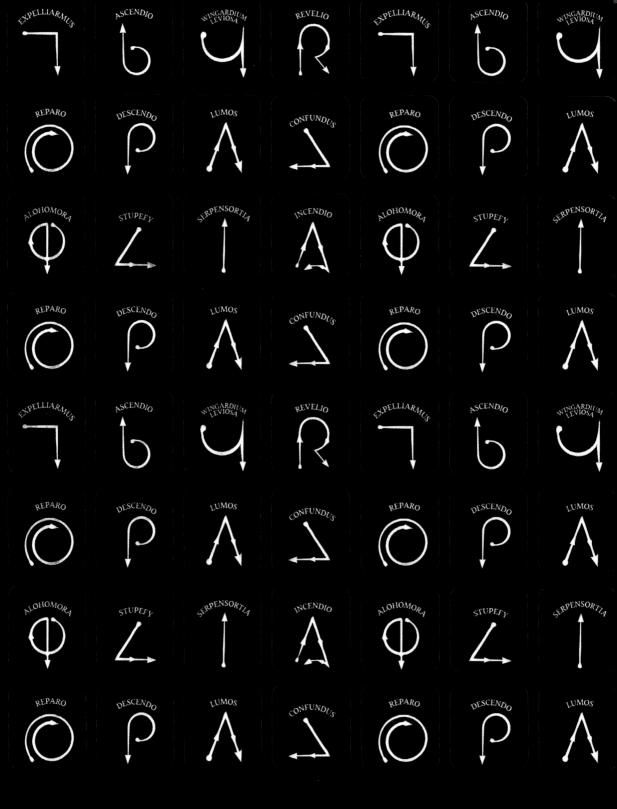

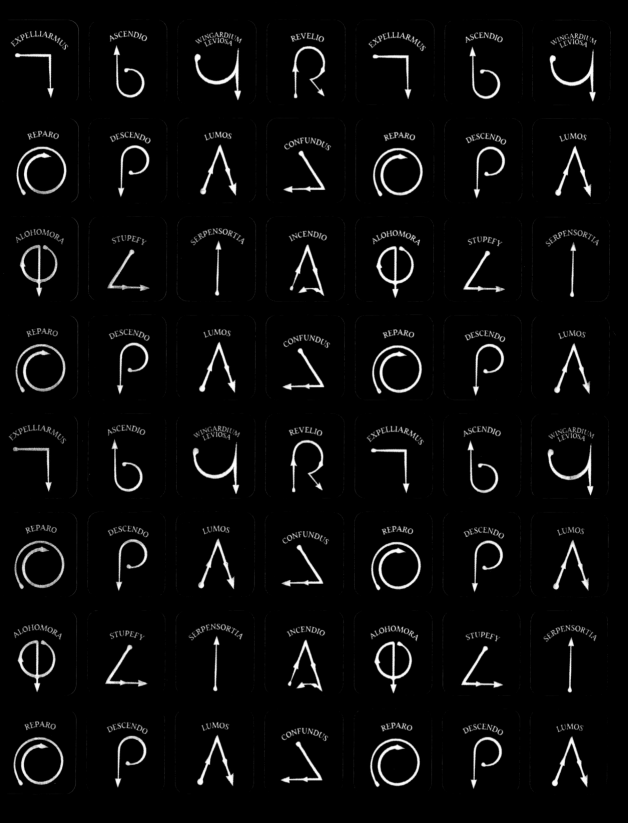

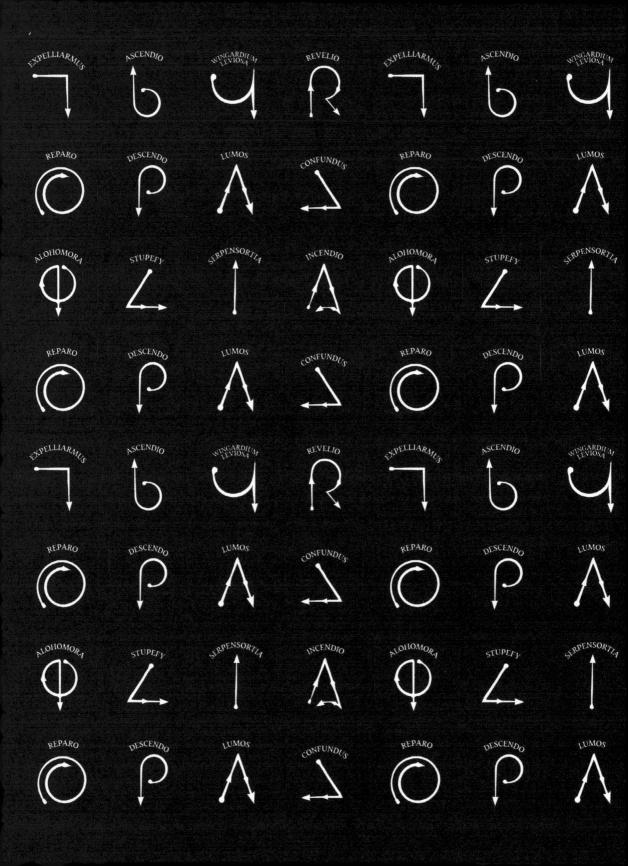

EXPELLIARMUS ASCENDIO WINGARDIUM LEVIOSA REVELIO EXPELLIARMUS ASCENDIO WINGARDIUM LEVIOSA

REPARO DESCENDO LUMOS CONFUNDUS REPARO DESCENDO LUMOS

ALOHOMORA STUPEFY SERPENSORTIA INCENDIO ALOHOMORA STUPEFY SERPENSORTIA

REPARO DESCENDO LUMOS CONFUNDUS REPARO DESCENDO LUMOS

EXPELLIARMUS ASCENDIO WINGARDIUM LEVIOSA REVELIO EXPELLIARMUS ASCENDIO WINGARDIUM LEVIOSA

REPARO DESCENDO LUMOS CONFUNDUS REPARO DESCENDO LUMOS

ALOHOMORA STUPEFY SERPENSORTIA INCENDIO ALOHOMORA STUPEFY SERPENSORTIA

REPARO DESCENDO LUMOS CONFUNDUS REPARO DESCENDO LUMOS

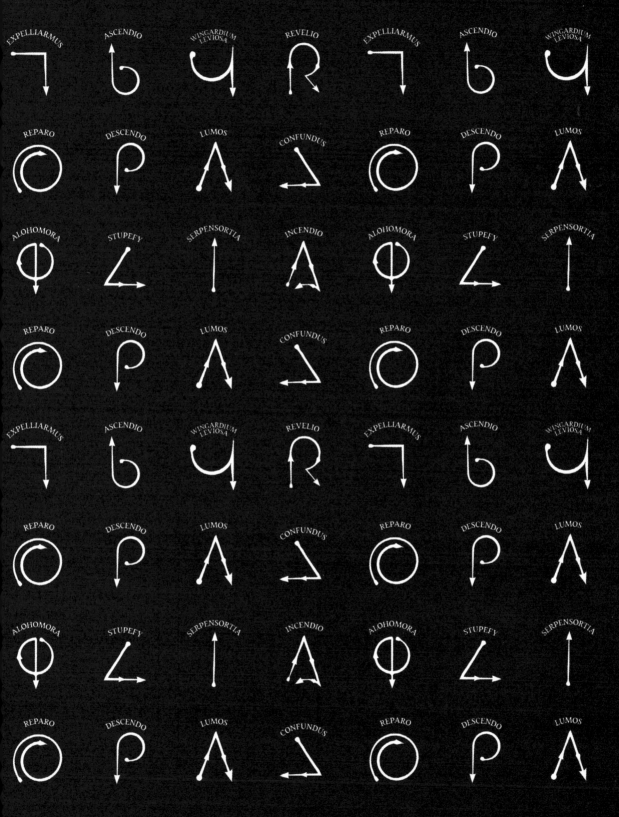

GRYFFINDOR

COURAGE — BRAVERY

DETERMINATION

RAVENCLAW

LEARNING

WISDOM — WIT

HUFFLEPUFF

DEDICATION

PATIENCE — LOYALTY

SLYTHERIN

CUNNING — PRIDE

AMBITION

GRYFFINDOR

COURAGE — BRAVERY

DETERMINATION

RAVENCLAW

WISDOM — WIT

LEARNING

WE ARE ONLY AS **STRONG** AS WE ARE **UNITED**

DUMBLEDORE'S ARMY

D.tt

HUFFLEPUFF

SLYTHERIN

CUNNING — PRIDE

AMBITION

G

GRYFFINDOR

R

RAVENCLAW

H

HUFFLEPUFF

S

SLYTHERIN

HOGWARTS

GRYFFINDOR

COURAGE — BRAVERY
DETERMINATION

RAVENCLAW

LEARNING
WISDOM — WIT

HUFFLEPUFF

DEDICATION
PATIENCE — LOYALTY

SLYTHERIN

CUNNING — PRIDE
AMBITION

GRYFFINDOR

COURAGE — BRAVERY
DETERMINATION

RAVENCLAW

WISDOM LEARNING WIT

WE ARE ONLY AS
STRONG
AS WE ARE
UNITED

DUMBLEDORE'S ARMY

DA

HUFFLEPUFF

SLYTHERIN

CUNNING AMBITION PRIDE

G
GRYFFINDOR

R
RAVENCLAW

H
HUFFLEPUFF

S
SLYTHERIN

HOGWARTS

G R H S

GRYFFINDOR
QUIDDITCH

TEAM · CAPTAIN

SLYTHERIN
QUIDDITCH

TEAM · CAPTAIN

HOGWARTS SCHOOL OF WITCHCRAFT & WIZARDRY

HUFFLEPUFF
QUIDDITCH

TEAM · CAPTAIN

RAVENCLAW
QUIDDITCH

TEAM · CAPTAIN

DUMBLEDORE'S ARMY

REDUCTO · EXPECTO
STUPEFY · PATRONUM

WE ARE ONLY
AS STRONG
AS WE ARE UNITED

HOGWARTS

BEAUTIFUL DAY FOR QUIDDITCH

SLYTHERIN

H

HUFFLEPUFF

RAVENCLAW

GRYFFINDOR

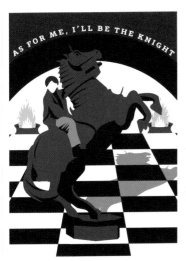

AS FOR ME, I'LL BE THE KNIGHT

ACCIO FIREBOLT!

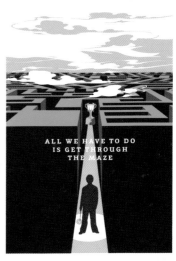

ALL WE HAVE TO DO
IS GET THROUGH
THE MAZE

GRYFFINDOR

HOGWARTS

BEAUTIFUL DAY FOR QUIDDITCH

SLYTHERIN

HUFFLEPUFF

RAVENCLAW

AS FOR ME, I'LL BE THE KNIGHT

ACCIO FIREBOLT!

ALL WE HAVE TO DO
IS GET THROUGH
THE MAZE

TRIWIZARD TOURNAMENT

DURMSTRANG

BEAUXBATONS

HOGWARTS

HARRY POTTER

CEDRIC DIGGORY

VIKTOR KRUM

FLEUR DELACOUR

TRIWIZARD TOURNAMENT

DURMSTRANG

BEAUXBATONS

HOGWARTS

HARRY POTTER

CEDRIC DIGGORY

VIKTOR KRUM

FLEUR DELACOUR

HOGWARTS

DRACO DORMIENS NUNQUAM TITILLANDUS

COURAGE
DETERMINATION
BRAVERY

AMBITION
PRIDE
CUNNING

LEARNING
WIT
WISDOM

PATIENCE
DEDICATION
LOYALTY

HOGWARTS

DRACO DORMIENS NUNQUAM TITILLANDUS

COURAGE
DETERMINATION
BRAVERY

AMBITION
PRIDE
CUNNING

LEARNING
WIT
WISDOM

PATIENCE
DEDICATION
LOYALTY

HAPPY CHRISTMAS!

HAPPY CHRISTMAS!

HAPPY CHRISTMAS!

HARRY POTTER

I'D RATHER STAY AT HOGWARTS THIS CHRISTMAS

HAPPY HOLIDAYS

YULE BALL HOGWARTS YULE BALL YULE HOGWARTS YULE BALL HOGWARTS YULE BALL YULE HOGWARTS

HAPPY CHRISTMAS!

HAPPY CHRISTMAS!

HAPPY CHRISTMAS!

HARRY POTTER

I'D RATHER STAY

AT HOGWARTS THIS CHRISTMAS

HAPPY HOLIDAYS

YULE BALL
HOGWARTS
YULE BALL YULE
HOGWARTS
YULE BALL
HOGWARTS
YULE BALL YULE
HOGWARTS

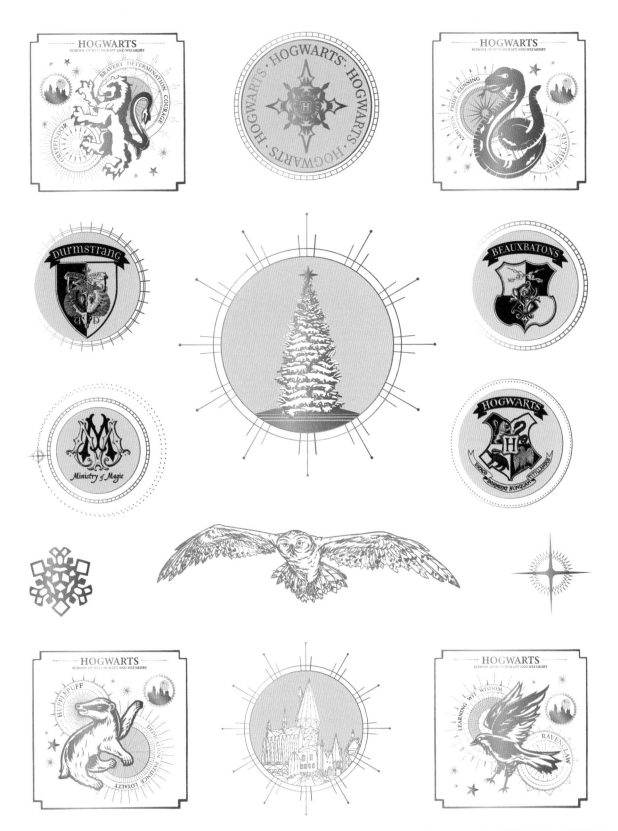

GRYFFINDOR

HUFFLEPUFF

RAVENCLAW

SLYTHERIN

HOGWARTS
SCHOOL OF
WITCHCRAFT AND WIZARDRY

YULE
BALL

YULE BALL

HOGWARTS
SCHOOL OF
WITCHCRAFT AND WIZARDRY

YULE BALL

YULE BALL

ALL I WANT FOR CHRISTMAS
NIMBUS 2000
THE GOLDEN SNITCH
WAND
SOCKS
CHOCOLATE FROG

ALL I WANT FOR CHRISTMAS

NIMBUS 2000

THE GOLDEN SNITCH

WAND

SOCKS

CHOCOLATE FROG

HOGWARTS

SCHOOL OF
WITCHCRAFT & WIZARDRY
TOGETHER WITH THE

MINISTRY OF MAGIC

REQUEST

THE PLEASURE
OF YOUR
COMPANY

AT THE

YULE BALL

STRICTLY DRESS TO IMPRESS
SEE PROFESSOR MCGONAGALL
FOR MORE DETAILS

DRACO DORMIENS NUNQUAM TITILLANDUS

HOGWARTS

SCHOOL OF
WITCHCRAFT & WIZARDRY
TOGETHER WITH THE

MINISTRY OF MAGIC

REQUEST

THE **PLEASURE**
OF YOUR
COMPANY

AT THE

YULE BALL

STRICTLY DRESS TO IMPRESS
SEE PROFESSOR MCGONAGALL
FOR MORE DETAILS

GRYFFINDOR

SLYTHERIN

HOGWARTS

HUFFLEPUFF

RAVENCLAW

DOBBY

GRYFFINDOR

HOGWARTS

· DRACO ·

· DORMIENS NUNQUAM ·

· TITILLANDUS ·

SLYTHERIN

HUFFLEPUFF

RAVENCLAW

GRYFFINDOR

SLYTHERIN

HOGWARTS

HUFFLEPUFF

RAVENCLAW

DOBBY

HOGWARTS

GRYFFINDOR

SLYTHERIN

· DRACO · DORMIENS NUNQUAM · TITILLANDUS ·

HUFFLEPUFF

RAVENCLAW

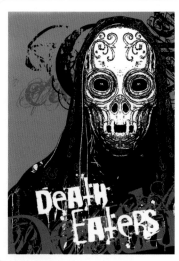

HOGSMEADE

WISEACRE'S WIZARDING EQUIPMENT

ZONKO'S

WEASLEY

OWL POST

DIAGON ALLEY

GRINGOTTS

Makers of Fine Wands

since 382 B.C.

FLOURISH AND BLOTTS

Bookseller

BORGIN & BURKES

HOGSMEADE

MINISTRY OF MAGIC

Wiseacre's WIZARDING EQUIPMENT

THE THREE BROOMSTICKS.

the Forbidden Forest

No. 257
for ONE WAY travel
LONDON TO HOGWARTS
Platform 9¾

The Leaky Cauldron

Wiseacre's Wizarding Equipment

PLATFORM 9¾
HOGWARTS EXPRESS

DIAGON ALLEY

BORGIN & BURKES

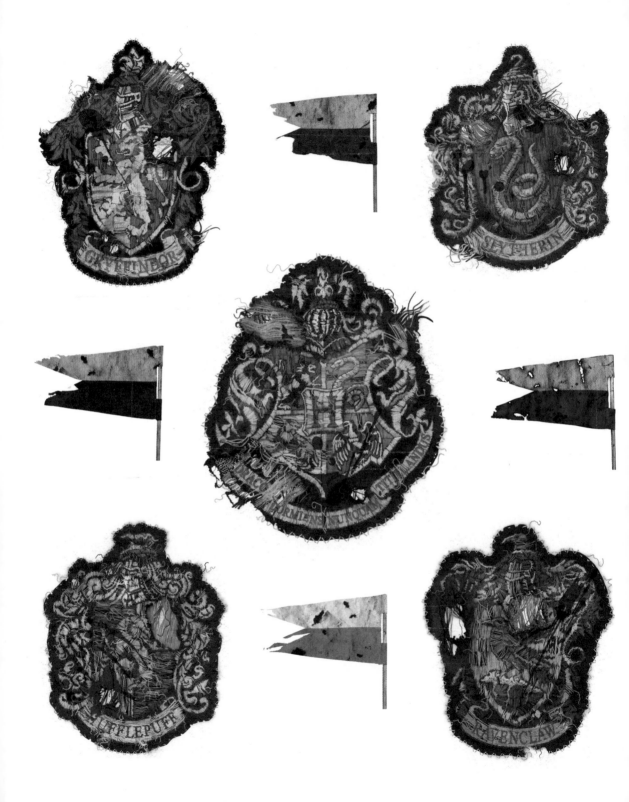

Owl post office
Owl post office

Dumbledore's D.A

Dumbledore's Army
D.A

ORDER

OF THE PHOENIX

Harry Potter

Ron Weasley

Hermione Granger

Luna Lovegood

Ginny Weasley

Neville Longbottom

Dumbledore's Army

D.A.

Hermione Granger

Ron Weasley

Harry Potter

George Weasley

Fred Weasley

Ginny Weasley

Luna Lovegood

Neville Longbottom

Padma Patil

Parvati Patil

Cho Chang

Zacharias Smith

Seamus Finnigan

Marietta Edgecombe

Katie Bell

Hannah Abbott

Susan Bones

Ernie Macmillan

ORDER
OF THE PHOENIX

Dumbledore's Army

D.A.

Harry Potter

Ron Weasley

Hermione Granger

Luna Lovegood

Ginny Weasley

Neville Longbottom

IGNORANTIA JURIS NEMINEM EXCUSAT

Dumbledore's DArmy

MINISTRY OF MAGIC

Hermione Granger
Ron Weasley
Harry Potter
George Weasley
Fred Weasley
Ginny Weasley
Luna Lovegood
Neville Longbottom
Padma Patil
Parvati Patil
Cho Chang
Zacharias Smith
Seamus Finnigan
Marietta Edgecombe
Katie Bell
Hannah Abbott
Susan Bones
Ernie Macmillan

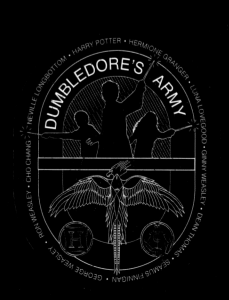

DUMBLEDORE'S ARMY

NEVILLE LONGBOTTOM • HARRY POTTER • HERMIONE GRANGER • LUNA LOVEGOOD • GINNY WEASLEY • DEAN THOMAS • SEAMUS FINNIGAN • GEORGE WEASLEY • RON WEASLEY • CHO CHANG •

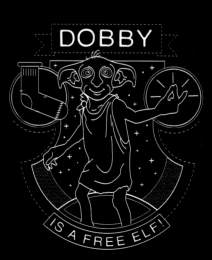

DOBBY

IS A FREE ELF!

DEATHLY HALLOWS

EXPECTO PATRONUM!

MORSMORDRE · DARK MARK · MORSMORDRE · DARK MARK · MORSMORDRE · DARK MARK

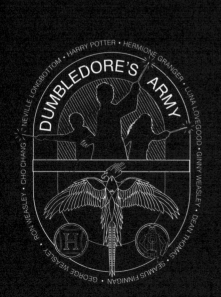

DUMBLEDORE'S ARMY

HARRY POTTER • HERMIONE GRANGER • LUNA LOVEGOOD • DEAN THOMAS • SEAMUS FINNIGAN • GINNY WEASLEY • GEORGE WEASLEY • RON WEASLEY • CHO CHANG • NEVILLE LONGBOTTOM

DOBBY

IS A FREE ELF!

DEATHLY ✦ HALLOWS

EXPECTO PATRONUM!

MORSMORDRE · DARK MARK

MORSMORDRE · DARK MARK

SEEKER

BRAVE AT HEART • DARING • NERVE • CHIVALRY • DETERMINATION

GRYFFINDOR

forbidden forest

EXPECTO PATRONUM!

FORTUNA MAJOR

DEATHLY   HALLOWS

Lumos

SLYTHERIN

GRYFFINDOR

QUIDDITCH

HUFFLEPUFF

RAVENCLAW

RAVENCLAW

BAD CROOKSHANKS

HUFFLEPUFF

THE MONSTER BOOK of MONSTERS

QUIDDITCH

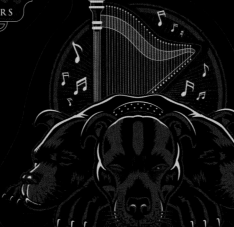

FLUFFY

GRYFFINDOR

SLYTHERIN

SLYTHERIN

GRYFFINDOR

QUIDDITCH

HUFFLEPUFF

RAVENCLAW

RAVENCLAW

BAD CROOKSHANKS

HUFFLEPUFF

THE MONSTER

BOOK of MONSTERS

QUIDDITCH

FLUFFY

GRYFFINDOR

SLYTHERIN

HufflePuff

DEDICATION
PATIENCE × LOYALTY

Gryffindor

DETERMINATION
COURAGE × BRAVERY

Hogwarts

SCHOOL OF
WITCHCRAFT & WIZARDRY

Ravenclaw

LEARNING
WIT × WISDOM

Slytherin

AMBITION × PRIDE × CUNNING

Marauder's Map

I SOLEMNLY SWEAR THAT I AM UP TO NO GOOD

Mischief Managed

Exceptionally Ordinary

Luna Lovegood

Mischief Managed

HufflePuff

DEDICATION
PATIENCE × LOYALTY

Gryffindor

DETERMINATION
COURAGE × BRAVERY

Hogwarts

SCHOOL OF
WITCHCRAFT & WIZARDRY

Ravenclaw

LEARNING
WIT × WISDOM

Slytherin

AMBITION × PRIDE × CUNNING

Marauder's Map

I SOLEMNLY SWEAR THAT I AM UP TO NO GOOD

Mischief Managed

EXceptionally Ordinary

Luna Lovegood

Mischief Managed

Thunder Bay Press
An imprint of Printers Row Publishing Group
9717 Pacific Heights Blvd, San Diego, CA 92121
www.thunderbaybooks.com • mail@thunderbaybooks.com

Printers Row Publishing Group is a division of Readerlink Distribution Services, LLC.
Thunder Bay Press is a registered trademark of Readerlink Distribution Services, LLC.

Correspondence regarding the content of this book should be sent to Thunder Bay Press, Editorial Department, at the above address.

Thunder Bay Press
Publisher: Peter Norton
Associate Publisher: Ana Parker
Art Director: Charles McStravick
Senior Developmental Editor: Diane Cain
Editor: Jessica Matteson
Designer: Brianna Lewis
Editorial Assistant: Sarah Hillberg
Production Team: Mimi Oey, Rusty von Dyl

ISBN: 978-1-6672-0544-1

Printed, manufactured, and assembled in Dongguan, China

27 26 25 24 23   2 3 4 5 6